Mozambique
MOMENTS

2002-3 NMI
MISSION EDUCATION RESOURCES

✳ ✳ ✳

READING BOOKS

ADVENTURE WITH GOD
The Jeanine van Beek Story
by Helen Temple

HANDS FOR THE HARVEST
Laborers for the Lord in the Far East
by A. Brent Cobb

JOURNEY TO JERUSALEM
Making a Difference in the Middle East
by Pat Stockett Johnston

MOZAMBIQUE MOMENTS
E-mail from the African Bush
by Douglas J. Perkins and Phyllis H. Perkins

TRIUMPH IN TRINIDAD
God's Promises Never Failed
by Ruth O. Saxon

UNDER THE "L"
Mission Field Chicago
by L. Wayne Hindmand

✳ ✳ ✳

ADULT MISSION EDUCATION RESOURCE BOOK

CALLED TO TEACH
Edited by Wes Eby

Mozambique MOMENTS
E-mail from the African Bush

DOUGLAS J. PERKINS & PHYLLIS H. PERKINS

Nazarene Publishing House
Kansas City, Missouri

Copyright 2002
by Nazarene Publishing House

ISBN 083-411-9617

Printed in the United States of America

Editor: Wes Eby
Cover Design: Michael Walsh

10   9   8   7   6   5   4   3   2   1

Dedicated to

Three missionary kids—
Marie, Elise, and Joanna—
who grew up in Central America,
South America, and Africa
and
their grandfather, Dr. Floyd J. Perkins,
retired missionary
from Mozambique, South Africa, and Brazil,
who started this continuing missionary cycle

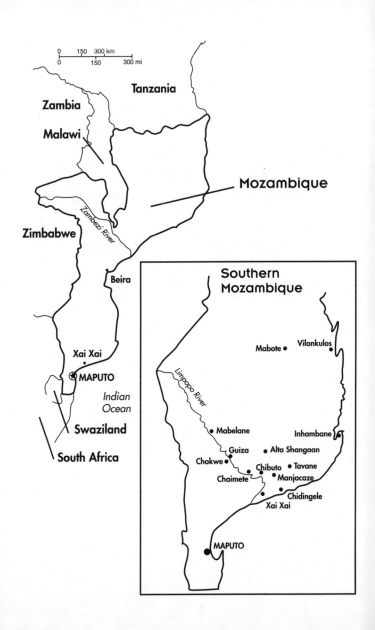

Contents

Doug Perkins and his wife, Elaine, are career missionaries for the Church of the Nazarene. Currently they are serving in Mozambique on the Africa Region, beginning this assignment in 1993. They are involved in pastoral education, the *JESUS* film ministry, and compassionate ministry activities. Previously, they were missionaries in Argentina and Uruguay in the South America Region for seven years.

Doug received the B.A. degree in religion from Northwest Nazarene College (now University) and the M.Div. degree from Nazarene Theological Seminary in Kansas City. The Perkinses have pastored in Missouri, Minnesota, and Oregon.

Doug is an MK (missionary kid), as his parents, Floyd and Libby Perkins, were Nazarene missionaries in Mozambique, South Africa, and Brazil.

The Perkinses have three grown daughters and two sons-in-law: Marie and Jason Benton, Elise and David Mosher, and Joanna.

Phyllis H. Perkins has devoted her life to missions and education in the Church of the Nazarene. Her varied assignments have included the following: missionary to Japan for five years; general NWMS (now NMI) director from 1980 to 1985; vice president for academic affairs, director of admissions, and professor at Nazarene Bible College from 1985 to 1998; professor at Northwest Nazarene College (now University); and adjunct professor at Nazarene Theological Seminary.

Phyllis has earned business education degrees from Northwest Nazarene College (B.A.), Oregon State University (M.Ed.), and Arizona State University (Ed.D.). She is an ordained elder in the Church of the Nazarene.

She is married to Dr. Floyd Perkins, former professor at Nazarene Bible College and missionary. In retirement, the Perkinses stay busy with speaking engagements. In addition, Phyllis is president of the Los Angeles District NMI.

Dr. Perkins is author of the 1994-95 NWMS (now NMI) reading book *Women in Nazarene Missions: Embracing the Legacy.* She also wrote *The Bible Speaks to Me About My Service and Mission* and *Together in Ministry,* the latter coauthored with her husband.

Introduction

$\mathcal{M}$y first picture of Mozambique came through the tiny window of a chartered eight-passenger plane, June 13, 1987. My husband, Floyd, and I had taken off from the Manzini,* Swaziland, airport; and just 30 minutes later we landed at Maputo, the capital of Mozambique. From the air, Maputo looked almost like any other modern city. The brilliant blue of the Indian Ocean accented the white buildings of the skyline along the smooth, sandy beaches. However, as the plane approached the tarmac, the stark reality of the 20-year civil war became apparent. The roofs of those once beautiful buildings were caving in, windows no longer in place. Few cars were on the streets of that city of more than 2 million people. The airport seemed nearly deserted. Yet, in the midst of desolate surroundings in one of the poorest countries in the world, a group of Shangaan Nazarenes rushed to greet and enfold us.

Nearly 35 years before, Floyd and Libby Perkins and their two small sons, Doug and David, had arrived in Lourenço Marques (now Maputo) to begin the work of the Church of the Nazarene among the Portuguese people. A daughter, Sheryl, joined the family two years later. As the children grew up in Mozambique and South Africa, Doug felt a call to mission service.

The stages of Doug's preparation included North-

---

*A guide on page 87 provides pronunciation of unfamiliar words in this book.

west Nazarene College (now University) where he met and married Elaine Finkbeiner; his seminary days in Kansas City where their first daughter, Marie, was born; their first pastorate in Portland, Oreg., where Elise joined the family; a year of language study in Costa Rica where Joanna arrived; and their years as missionaries in Argentina and Uruguay. All these assignments were preliminary to their present ministry in Mozambique. Even their first term as missionaries in Mozambique was basically without communication with no convenient access to a local telephone, fax, or the Internet.

During their furlough year of 1998-99, Doug made swift connection with a cell phone, laptop computer, and digital camera. Then, the Mozambique story from his perspective began to emerge from his E-mail server to a growing list of family and supporters around the world. Those folks were impacted to pray with new meaning, give with greater sacrifice, challenge young people, and, in some cases, go themselves on Work and Witness teams. Moreover, some receiving the E-mails began to voice the hope that the global Nazarene family could be given the opportunity to look over Doug and Elaine's shoulders to learn what God is doing in Mozambique at the turn of the new century. That is the purpose of this book—to connect you with some of the miraculous story that God is writing in Mozambique as reported by Doug Perkins via technology.

To allow for as much of the story as possible, the usual greetings and signatures have been omitted, and many E-mails have been abridged.

Phyllis H. Perkins, Doug's second mom

1

Merry Christmas

*C*hristmas Day 1995 dawned bright and beautiful in Xai Xai, Mozambique, where my retired missionary husband and I were visiting our son Doug, his wife, Elaine, and two of their three teenage daughters, Elise and Joanna. At 7:00 A.M. the hot, sultry atmosphere was already bearing down on us as Elaine came down the hall announcing, "I have sunshine, water, and electricity. I'm going to do laundry." We all scrambled for our dirty clothes, knowing that sunshine, water, and electricity were unpredictable commodities in that missionary home and not to be wasted for a moment—not even on Christmas morning.

Later in the day, we drove to the only hotel in the area that had reopened since the 20-year civil war. The food was disappointing, but the setting was breathtaking. We were seated outdoors within steps of the sloping, white-sand beach and the sparkling waves of the Indian Ocean. Paradise! Or paradise lost? The latter seemed a more appropriate description as Doug wrote about Christmas in Mozambique a few years later. He was writing

to family and friends from his furlough reveries, re-
minding us what Christmas truly signifies.

October 15, reflections while on furlough. . . . Last Christmas, Elaine, Joanna, and I were in Mozambique. It was a bright, clear, and *very* hot day. Heat waves undulating from the surface of the national highway distorted distant trees. Palm trees seemed to wiggle their way up toward bright cumulonimbus clouds. They were monstrous white clouds, puffing their way up into the stratosphere.

Joanna and I had attended morning services and then headed out for the beach. Driving 14 kilometers (8.5 miles), we crested a hill and came into full view of the magnificent, blue Indian Ocean. Putting on fins and snorkels, we swam out to the coral reef 50 yards from the shore. We watched as parrot fish swam lazily over orange and white coral. Joanna pointed ahead at zebra fish. An eel slithered off to the right. Three hours of snorkeling went by in 10 minutes.

Climbing the dunes, we made our way back to the truck parked in the shade of a large mafureira tree. We found a lad sitting on the back bumper, staring down at the sand and drawing pictures with his feet. He looked up tentatively, as though he were afraid of us. He rose from the bumper and moved away from the truck.

"Wait," Joanna smiled and called out to the lad. He stopped and looked fully at us. Then we saw it. He had been burned horribly, and scars covered one side of his face, shoulder, and arm.

"Please, Sir, I'm hungry." Joanna looked at me. I turned to get in the truck. "Dad, didn't you hear? This boy is hungry. Can't we give him something?"

I gave Joanna some money. Suddenly a huge smile came to the boy's face. He turned and started to run. "Wait," I called to him. He stopped. "What are you going to do with the money?"

"I'm going to buy bread. I've got brothers and sisters who're hungry."

"Merry Christmas," we called after him.

He turned back to face us. "Merry Christmas," he smiled, raising his arm to wave. He had no hand; the fire had burned it off.

"Dad, if it pains our hearts so, it must really pain God's heart."

Joanna looked at me, large tears filling her eyes. "Dad," she said, "in this world there is beauty and goodness, and there is so much that is tragic and sad and ugly. I hate it!"

We sat silently in the truck, looking out across the blue ocean. "Jo," I broke the silence, "God hates it too. That's why He sent Jesus."

She nodded in agreement. "Dad, if it pains our hearts so, it must really pain God's heart."

The words of a song flashed across my mind. One line goes, "Wherever human hearts and human woes abound." Then the refrain resounds, "The Comforter has come! / The Comforter has come!"

And He propels us. He propels us out to make a difference. He propels us out with the message of Jesus. He propels us out with the message about bread—the Bread of Life. After all, we are just beggars telling other beggars where to get the Bread. . . .

Elaine and I are preparing to return to Mozambique on March 29 [1999]. The needs are great, but the resources are few. Yet, we are looking forward to our return with great anticipation—anticipation of the presence, direction, and leadership of the Holy Spirit. His resources are limitless and immediately available. We go with His joy. We'll be leaving our daughters behind, but we were never sorry they were exposed to Christmas in Mozambique. They needed to know that most of the world lives in poverty, sin, and degradation. They needed to know that Christmas really is about Jesus and the joy that He brings.

Christmas is all about the Bread, giving it out and telling others where to find it. . . .

2

Farewell and Welcome

A s their furlough year of 1998-99 was end-
ing, Doug and Elaine's E-mail messages
sent to family reflected both their sorrow at leaving
family and their anticipation of returning to
Mozambique for their second term of missionary
service in Africa.

March 17, Olathe, Kansas. . . . Elaine and I are in
our final week and a half of furlough, and a year ago
this point seemed quite a long way off. Upon our return to Africa we will be

- Looking for and purchasing a four-door, four-
wheel-drive pickup in Maputo.
- Setting up our house in Xai Xai for the next three
years.
- Traveling to Tavane (three hours from Xai Xai) to
assess the medical needs and begin a project . . . to
get water up the Tavane Hill, feeding into large
storage tanks. The villagers and clinic will then
have water . . . now they carry it on their heads for
quite a distance.
- Traveling to all 19 Bible training centers to assess
their needs, preach, teach, and deliver supplies.

- Traveling to 10 district assemblies during the month of May, some in remote areas. One will be in the Alta Shangaan area. In 1997 while traveling in this area for a wedding, many snakes were seen crossing the road, including a large mamba and a python. The Mozambicans with us were very afraid, as sighting snakes is a bad omen.

Sandy, dirt road in Alta Shangaan

- Visiting the gold mines in June, holding evangelistic meetings among the Mozambican miners, and bringing their tithes back to their respective churches.
- Traveling to a church leaders' conference in Johannesburg, 12 hours away . . . and being responsible for getting four or five Mozambican district superintendents and their wives to this conference, along with securing passports, visas, and bus tickets.
- Overseeing the printing of a programmed Wesleyan theology textbook, which I'm hoping to use

in our pastoral and lay training program.

- Purchasing and distributing Bibles and hymnals and other Christian literature in our area.
- Coordinating medical teams coming into Mozambique. The life expectancy in our area is 42 years for males and 48 years for females. Meds are very crucial, especially Tylenol, Chloroquine (for malaria), vitamins, tropical skin creams, and antiworm medicines.
- Preparing for Work and Witness teams coming to Xai Xai.
- Preparing teams to use the *JESUS* film and conduct follow-up and discipleship classes.

Please be in prayer for us as we depart. It will be most difficult to say our good-byes; but, on the other hand, our friends and relatives and children can be involved in all of the ministry in Mozambique through prayer. Prayer not only moves mountains but also is the vehicle upon which the work of Jesus advances around the world. . . .

I could read it in her tear-filled eyes, silent words that touched my heart— a quiet thank-you.

I cannot forget the eyes of an elderly 84-year-old Mozambican woman. The American doctors had helped her after she had been severely beaten by her own family for being a witch. Her only failing was being old and displaying the familiar symptoms of old age. Her skin peeling off, she was broken, bruised, and battered. There was not a quarter of an inch of undamaged skin left on her body. Her gnarled, bony hand reached out and grasped mine, and I could read it in her tear-filled eyes, silent words that touched my heart—a quiet thank-you. And so let me give to you her words—our thank-you for caring.

A last weekend in Kansas City brought family and friends together. Doug and Elaine's eldest daughter, Marie, and her husband, Jason, lived in nearby Olathe. Their middle daughter, Elise, and her new husband, David, as well as their youngest daughter, Joanna, drove up from Bethany, Oklahoma. Elaine's family flew in from Washington State. We all finally gathered at the airport. Charles Gailey, Nazarene Theological Seminary professor of missions and former missionary to Africa, and his wife, Doris, prayed for us in a sacred circle before we embraced Doug and Elaine and bravely waved good-bye. We watched the plane until it disappeared into the clouds. We wiped our tears and waited for the next communication. It came later that night from the Minneapolis airport where Doug framed his feelings and thoughts in a final stateside message.

March 29, Minneapolis. . . . This will be our final communication from this E-mail address. It has been a long, arduous journey across the United States, crossing the continent several times. There have been some difficult times, and there have been moments when we felt we could not go on for another minute. We were drained physically and emotionally, but never spiritually. . . . The hardest thing for us is saying good-bye to everyone, especially to our youngest child. But we leave her in the care of our Lord. . . .

> *Then Doug and Elaine canceled the Internet service and flew to Africa in God's will. We waited for that first electronic link, saying they had arrived safely. They borrowed other missionaries' computers to share with us those first hours and days "back home" in Africa.*

March 31, Johannesburg. . . . Elaine and I arrived safely but tired in Johannesburg early this morning. Jim and Arlajean Buchanan, two of their children, and Ken Walker, our field director, were there to meet us.

We then picked up our airfreight, which was a process of three hours—shuttling back and forth between buildings and trying to collect all of the signatures and stamps. Ken was patient enough to take us back and forth. It was a process, but welcome to Africa! Then, the Buchanans' pickup refused to start, so we had to push-start it. Welcome to Africa! Next the inspector had to examine our luggage, and we had to pick him up and take him to the trunks. Welcome to Africa!

Today we went over to the regional office and squared some things away to be able to buy a vehicle, bed, and stove next week. Tomorrow we start out for Manzini [Swaziland], sleep there tomorrow night, and move on to Maputo the next day. We're hoping for no trouble at the border. Friday will be a zoo at the border, as Easter is a big tourist weekend in Mozambique with lines of cars one or two miles long, waiting to cross the frontier [border]. . . .

April 2, Maputo. . . . Elaine and I crossed the Mozambique frontier at approximately 11:30 A.M. today. We had 12 pieces of luggage; 4 were footlockers with a scanner in one. But we made it though without any trouble after the customs officials had inspected everything. We prayed all night, and you must have been praying too! . . . Monday, I will definitely be on-line with my own computer, I hope! . . .

April 6, Maputo. . . . We are finally on-line with Tropical Net, a server here in Maputo. . . .

April 8, Maputo. . . . Elaine and I are enjoying this E-mail connection. We're still in Maputo, but that's par for the course in Mozambique. We're reorienting ourselves to "everything is a process, and there is always tomorrow." It takes time to do anything here. So you better make friends with time. Hopefully, we'll get our vehicle today, but then we'll have a ton of paperwork to do. . . .

April 9, Maputo. . . . Today was a day of miracles. Doors opened and closed. People all moved, spoke, and acted under the sovereign hand of our loving

Heavenly Father. Tomorrow we are on to Xai Xai where we've heard the people are expecting us. . . . Truly, God's mighty hand was upon us, and we're looking for a tremendous three years of God's sovereign leadership. . . .

Doug at his computer, sending E-mails from the African bush

At Home in Xai Xai

X ai Xai, located about 230 kilometers (140 miles) north of Maputo, is where Doug and Elaine served during their first mission term in Mozambique. Known as a resort town in pre-civil war days, its Indian Ocean beach could compete with any in Hawaii, the Caribbean, or the South Sea Islands. Gradually, the area is recovering and rebuilding, but progress is slow in a country where the infrastructure was virtually destroyed.

Finding adequate housing in 1994 when Doug and Elaine first arrived was difficult. With the help of Jim Williams, a mission volunteer, they remodeled a warehouse and added a kitchen. Finally, just as they were ready for furlough, their new house was ready for occupancy. Perhaps the most welcomed benefit was a telephone with a dial tone. That had taken three years.

Doug's E-mails relate their first days back in Xai Xai.

April 10, Xai Xai. . . . Elaine and I have finally arrived in Xai Xai. It's a relief to be home, but we're seeing how much the house was neglected while

22

gone for one year. . . . We don't have a key to the storeroom where our belongings are and, therefore, cannot unpack anything. We have no fridge, no generator, no washing machine. I'm trying to get the key from another missionary, but he lives 140 miles away. At the moment Elaine is scrubbing countertops, and is it ever hot! We aren't used to this heat anymore. We'll have to become acclimated again. . . .

Doug and Elaine's home in Xai Xai

April 13, Xai Xai. . . . The unpacking began today. This morning the key to the locked storeroom arrived. . . . So, Elaine and I have spent the day beginning to unpack—sort of. Halfway through we received visitors. One of them is a young pastor from Inhambane who was recently ordained and married.

. . . Then I picked about 40 ticks off Fritz, our German shepherd, and sprayed him down with antitick medicines. I then made a backup copy of my hard drive, just in case the whole system crashes. I then found a new control mechanism for the washing machine and installed it. Next, I tackled the alarm system on the car. During all of this, I helped Elaine with some box moving. Jose Langa, our guard, was also helping her so that I could get some of this other stuff done. . . .

Sunday we went to visit Rev. Benjamin Langa, and he related the story of his stroke and wife's death. She died a painful death from liver cancer. Benjamin has partially recovered from his stroke and can get around with some difficulty. . . .

So goes the battle. But in the meantime, we're having fun working for Jesus here in Gaza [Province]. . . .

This E-mail message of April 24 was sent to their mailing list. It describes more of their cultural reentry to Mozambique.

April 24, Xai Xai. . . . Just a quick note to let you know that Elaine and I are back in Mozambique after one year of furlough. Although we live 230 kilometers (140 miles) north of Maputo, we are on-line, so feel free to E-mail us at any time. . . .

Elaine and I went into town, which is four kilometers (2.5 miles) away, and were astounded by the sights and smells and the tremendous need all around. We saw a 40-year-old man who from his head down to his waist was normal in physiology. But from his waist down, he had one short, thin 13-inch leg with a foot. He wore a sock and tennis shoe and walked about on crutches.

A beggar came up to us at the post office. "Missionary, I'm glad you're back."

A little farther down the street, we encountered a teenager, sitting in rags, bringing a plastic bottle up to his mouth and nose, sniffing. Saliva ran from the corners of his mouth. A beggar came up to us at the post office. "Missionary, I'm glad you're back," he said. His body was in the shape of the letter S. . . .

The workers at the post office all came out and greeted us. "We hope we'll deliver many letters to you," they said, laughing. It is their custom to come out and apologize on days when we have no mail as if it were somehow their fault. . . . This is the land where God has called us to serve.

We would like to thank you for your prayers and all your help during our furlough. Last week we purchased a pickup, bed, and stove. Sunday we initiated the truck by filling it with people and using the four-wheel drive to get us through 10 inches of sand on our way to church. All of these items will serve our ministry here as we labor for Christ and for you in the bush of Mozambique.

In just a week we'll start a circuit of visiting eight districts, meeting with the pastors, laypeople, and superintendents. These sessions will be times of inspiration, church business, and just listening. We will hear exciting stories—stories of how God has blessed and how the gospel has changed lives. We will hear sad stories—stories of need, physical, emotional, medical, and nutritional. The spiritual need is so great! . . .

4

To the Work,
to the Work

*T*he burdens and challenges of a needy people in a needy land are filtered to us through the eyes and hearts of missionaries on the front lines. Kingdom work claims Doug and Elaine's attention every waking moment and intrudes on their sleep. Doug electronically details their travels and triumphs, their frustrations and fears. Yet, in the midst of tremendous opportunities with limited time and resources, they—and we—hear the voice of God himself speak peace and comfort. We hear His words of guidance and direction. After all, it is His church in Mozambique, and He is the great Equipper of His missionaries and national leaders. Here are some excerpts from Doug's E-mails.

May 1, Xai Xai. . . . We're learning to live with deficiencies. We have electricity, which isn't stable, and sometimes we are without. We are learning to live without adequate water; we still have it, but not always. We are learning to live without a big supermarket close by. We go grocery shopping every three or four months. It's amazing how little a person can really live on. We have no television, and sometimes we can't even pick up a decent radio signal.

But we are learning to listen and hear the voice of our loving Savior who bids us to come to Him. We are enjoying the quiet nights and the bright stars of the Milky Way . . . the beach and the trees of the semiforested areas of Gaza. And we are enjoying the people.

God's Word has become ever so meaningful as we read together every day and have claimed Psalm 27 to guide us for this term of service. The needs are so huge. Theological education is a big need, as well as the need to study God's Word. People are so hungry for the Word. The other day an old pastor came and said, "Missionary, when you were gone, no one brought the Word to us. But now that you are here, please bring the Word back to us." . . .

May 10, Xai Xai. . . . Elaine and I are breathing and resting easier. We bought a large truck battery and now run all of our computer equipment off of it. I will recharge overnight. I have a backup battery left over from last term, which should work just fine. It's dangerous to operate electronic equipment off the open current here, as our power fluctuates so much. . . .

May 13, Xai Xai. . . . Elaine and I just returned from several days in the bush and enjoyed every minute of it. We were in Tavane, Mavengane, Chibuto, Chokwe, Xai Xai, Zavala, Inhambane, and Vilankulos. We were at the district assemblies in these eight places. . . . The assemblies went well, and we had terrific growth on many districts. One district grew by 140 percent, another by 41 percent, and yet another by 20 percent. Many people are coming to know Christ and are turning from darkness to light. . . .

Today while I sat out under the shade of a huge cashew tree, a little boy, Jaime, came to me. He was afraid at first, but then he came and leaned his body across my legs. He was frail and thin. His hair had a reddish tinge, the telltale sign of malnutrition. "How old are you?" I asked. He looked down at the ground.

District assembly in Inhambane. *L. to r.:* Missionary Doug Perkins, Rev. Paul Sueia, and Rev. Jonas Mulate.

His mother standing nearby said, "He's four."

He looked up into my eyes and smiled. "Snake," he said, pointing up, and immediately I looked up.

His mother laughed. "Missionary," she said, "a month ago, we had a women's group from Maputo, and two snakes fell out of the tree right where you are sitting."

When nobody was looking, I changed my location. From then on Elaine and I watched the trees above us.

When we said our good-byes, the people began to weep. "Oh, missionary," they said, "this place has many witch doctors, and we are afraid." So after prayer and a hymn, we commended them to God's care and left for Xai Xai, promising them that we would return soon. . . .

I wonder if Handel ever thought the "Hallelujah Chorus" would be sung in the heart of the African bush.

May 20, Xai Xai. . . . Elaine and I have had an eventful day with various visitors, going into town to check the mail, buy dog food, and check on Bibles. Then tonight we had a scare—a huge power surge that may have affected the computer. Anyway, as the saying goes in Africa, if anything can go wrong, it went wrong yesterday. . . .

May 21, Xai Xai. . . . Sunday morning a youth choir at the Inhamissa church sang the "Hallelujah Chorus." Handel never sounded so good as it floated out over the great palms, reaching up to the skies, through the stately mango and cashew trees. All of the trees of the forest clapped their branches together as His reign was lauded forever and ever. I wonder if Handel ever thought the "Hallelujah Chorus" would be sung in the heart of the African bush. . . .

Nazarene congregation near Xai Xai

May 27, Xai Xai. . . . The day dawned dark. Clouds, heavy with rain, stretched from Xai Xai to beyond the distant hills. The green forest of cashew, mango, and mafureira trees stood quiet in the still air, sentinel to some greater event about to happen. Already in four-wheel drive, we negotiated several deep sandy areas where we were forced by the oncoming vehicles. They flick their lights at approaching traf-

fic, meaning "get off the road and let me through."
Off the road, you are in deep sand, and you had better have four-wheel drive or you will be stuck in
sand as deep as the axles.

This was Pentecost Sunday, and we were headed out to Manjacaze to preach. The skies suddenly
opened, and water came down in torrents. Deep
sand became deep mud. Lightning that started way
out in the distance began walking with jagged fingers
toward us. Like giant, gnarled fingers, it reached its
ragged hand, striking huge cashew trees, scorching
them, and setting them on fire. One flash sheared off
a branch, leaving it smoldering on the road.

Elaine was the first to speak, "Maybe we should
turn around. The lightning is coming toward us. It
will strike us. Or we will get stuck." Her hand was
trembling on my arm. *Maybe we should turn back*, I
thought for a while. *Maybe it's foolish to continue on.*

"On the other hand," my wife said, "maybe the
devil doesn't want us in Manjacaze." We prayed and
continued on with our journey, arriving around 9:30
A.M. The brothers and sisters, concerned for our safety, shouted for joy as we pulled into the churchyard.
They sang, waved their hands in the air, and praised
God. This would be a Pentecost to remember! The
Holy Spirit was there, protecting, uplifting, inspiring,
helping, comforting. The people sang an old song ti-
tled "Send Thy Blessing, Lord," one that we haven't
sung in the United States since the late 1800s or early 1900s.

Before the service, we had breakfast of fish
heads, lettuce, bread, fried eggs, and tea, eaten in a

neighbor's house because of the rain. The sun came out, and the dark rolling, boiling clouds lifted, revealing God's providence and grace to our hearts.

Isabel stood over by the cookhouse, three fingers in her mouth. This two-and-a-half-year-old, beautiful child with short hair had such a pained and puzzled look. "Whose child is this?" I asked, her pain touching my heart.

"Oh, this one," the pastor said. "Her mother died three days ago in childbirth. Her father left her with us."

We are not abandoned, even while the ragged fingers of evil ravage us.

And then I saw and understood it. She was abandoned, left alone. That look of pain, that look of abandonment, that look of destitution was utter aloneness. Its ragged hand grabbed my heart.

Easter was a great day. Christ overcame death. All of the suffering, sin, and oppression of the world was laid on Him, and He bore it all away. But we live with the reality of the conquered evil still trying to raise its vanquished head. I believe in the Resurrection. Without it we have no gospel at all. But Pentecost. Ah, Pentecost! Christ gave us a gift more precious—His Holy Spirit to be with us, alongside us, encouraging us. We are not abandoned, even while the ragged fingers of evil ravage us, leaving us afraid, doubting, alone.

Little Isabel came over to me, and I held her in my arms to comfort her—His Comfort. Having no mother that day, she searched for someone to bond to. Picking out a pastor, she sat with him through the service, clapping her hands while we sang "Send Thy Blessing, Lord." Many people came to the altar, seeking the blessed Holy Spirit and His sanctifying power.

"Who will take care of this little child?" I inquired.

"My wife and I," said the pastor. "She is already ours. We will look after her until she marries. We want to. It's no burden to us." His hand rested on her little head while she held on to his leg, her small hand gripping the cloth of his trousers and wrinkling it.

In late afternoon we pressed for home. Driving in four-wheel drive all of the way, we arrived after dark. I relaxed outside. Our electricity had vanished, which occurs frequently where we live. Millions—maybe billions—of stars lit up the dark skies.

"Are you there, Mufundisi (reverend)," a voice called out from the dark black of the night.

"Oh, yes, I am here."

"Did your day go well, Mufundisi?"

"Oh, yes, it went very well."

"Mufundisi, the road is long, and there is danger and much suffering."

"Yes, Bava (father)," I said, "the road is long, and there is much suffering."

"Mufundisi, my son came back from South Africa. He is sick with Slims (AIDS). Can you come tomorrow and pray with him? He is dying, and his mother's heart is stripped."

"Yes, Bava, I will come and pray with him and with inkosikasi (his mother)."

"Mufundisi, we are afraid."

"Yes, Bava, we can be afraid, but Jesus sends His Spirit."

"Yes, Mufundisi, He is the Greatest Gift."

"Goodnight, Mufundisi."

"Goodnight, my father."

The night was quiet. The Spirit is the Sign. We are wanted and not abandoned. . . .

5

Tavane Past and Present

*W*hen I stepped onto the Tavane property in 1995, I realized I was on sacred ground. Nazarene mission history rose up to meet me at every turn. I snapped photos of the house where Lorraine Schultz had lived. I gazed in awe at the huge coconut trees Oscar Stockwell had planted. I sipped tea in the house where Armand and Pauline Doll had lived, while I listened to African leaders tell stories about missionaries who had lived at Tavane and had impacted their lives. I walked thoughtfully to the Glenn Grose Memorial Church for an afternoon service and reveled in the blending of rich African voices as they sang familiar Christmas carols and offered fervent prayers. They had suffered and survived to herald and celebrate God's faithfulness. It's little wonder that Tavane figures largely in Doug's thoughts, plans, and travels.*

February 13, 1999, a reverie written by Doug while on furlough. . . . The sun, a giant red ball, hung suspended in a thick, gray stripe of smoke and cloud on the distant western horizon. Palm leaves crackled as they stirred in the light easterly breezes. The evening was cooling a little from the blasting heat and drooping humidity of the day. We sat on the veranda of what used to be the old Stockwell house, overcome by the sounds, sights, and smells of the African evenings. We were missionaries, doctors, dentists, and a college student resting from the pressure and emotions of the day's activities. This was Tavane.

Off in the distance we began to hear the rhythms of drums—demon drums. Over to the left, the music of voices sang beautifully in harmony. They were women's voices, lifting sweetly the strains of "What a Friend We Have in Jesus." Off to the north, the Glenn Grose Memorial Church stood illuminated, pink and orange in the last rays of a weakening sunlight. Tavane Hill was suddenly alive with voices of people long dead, threading their way through the coconut palms.

Later in the shimmering moonlight, I saw the Glenn Grose Memorial Church standing tall. It's a monument that bears witness to many people and events. First, to Glenn Grose who drowned after a trip to the leper colony. To Oscar Stockwell who knew Shangaan and preached the gospel for decades in Mozambique. To Lorraine Schultz, Mary Cooper, Leona Youngblood, Virginia Benedict, Pat Buffet, Minnie Martin—women who taught the love of Christ and gave their lives to care for the sick and dying, proclaiming God's grace in Christ Jesus. It bears witness to a Spirit-moving revival in 1958 where many of our present Mozambican leaders heard Christ's call and to the 1934 volunteer army of 10,000 Americans who gave $1 each to save the property. It bears witness to hundreds, if not thousands, of Mozambican Christians who lost their lives during the horrific civil war.

Glen Grose Memorial Church

That old building has withstood the ravages of war, wind, and torrential tropical storms. Holes were blasted into it by rocket and mortar fire. Wind has blown out all of the glass. Persons have stood on her steps and defiantly, arrogantly, but perhaps ignorantly, declared, "God is dead." Soldiers made it their headquarters, and others defiled and mocked it. But on any day of the week, you will hear the sound of jubilant voices singing. God is alive, and He has come to live among us. Let this incontrovertible news be heralded throughout the land. It calls from

Tavane Hill. This news calls to us from the Glenn Grose Memorial Church, but also from further back—from Calvary!

Faith through the night brings the miracle of the morning.

The wind rustles the palm branches. Katydids, locusts, and a million insects shrilly break the stillness of the night. One lonely lantern sits on a crude table in the house. We gaze at the bright starlight of the Milky Way and marvel at the mighty Hand that spread out this universe of light.

A voice calls to us from the night, "Please, send the doctor." A man has been brought to the clinic. He may die. The doctors grab their bags and flashlights and run through the bush. A man has been clubbed. He is bleeding. His family sits around him, moaning and crying out, "Will he live?" Staying with him throughout the night, we watch over the man until the sunrise on the eastern horizon. The first rays shoot across the Indian Ocean. Uninterrupted, they reach out across miles of bush and jungle, illuminating a church on Tavane Hill, bathing it in pink and orange and red. The family gathers. "He lives, he lives," they cry out. Faith through the night brings the miracle of the morning. . . .

Mozambique, a country of 18 million people, is experiencing a great turning to Christ. The Church of the Nazarene is growing at a rate of 15 new members per day. Every fourth day a new church is started. A volunteer army is needed. An army of prayer warriors and givers. An army of helpers, doctors, agronomists, teachers, pastors. An army of volunteers who will say to God, "Here am I, send me."

One day I was at the leper village now alongside Lake Chidingele. I met an elderly man whose fingers had worn down to stubs, his nose worn away. He reached out and hesitatingly, haltingly, touched my arm. I had asked if there was anyone who remembered an mufundisi, a missionary, Glenn Grose. "This Bible," he said, holding out a tattered old Bible, "it was given to me by Mufundisi Grose."

I opened this Holy Book. There I found a signature, a name, and an old, yellowed picture. "Yes," said the old man, "Mufundisi Grose came here to us with hope and light. Is there no one you can send to help us? Is there no one? . . ."

September 26, another reverie from the vantage point of furlough. . . . One hot night, I was sitting in the old Stockwell house on the Tavane mission station. Everyone else had gone to the district meetings except for a 64-year-old preacher named Francisco. Sitting in the dimly lit room, with frogs and crickets and other insects croaking, chirping, and whirring, Francisco related to me a deeply moving story.

His oldest daughter had been kidnapped by opposing forces during the civil war. She had escaped and then tried to get back to her parents' home. But she was caught again just 20 miles from home—just 20 miles from freedom. Taken back to the opposition's base, she was brutally murdered. Staked to the ground, her broken and abused body was hacked inch by inch until she was dead. This was done as an example to all who would try to escape.

Francisco and I sat there in the silence and darkness for the longest time. Tears flowed from our eyes. But then I heard a voice in the dark. Jesus, a totally innocent man, died on the Cross. On the third day He rose again from the dead. Because He rose again, we will rise to be with Him. And we will be whole. "I will see my daughter again, missionary."

Many people have lost loved ones, all of their possessions, or their health. Many die of diseases. Malaria is rampant, a killer not respecting age, color, or religion. Contracting cerebral malaria gives you 48 hours to find medicine to treat it. Most Mozambicans are thousands of kilometers from help.

Today, Elaine and I have the privilege of serving in this war-ravaged country. The average per capita income is $75 per year. We thought we would have found rather meager offerings and people complaining about having to give to the church. Instead we found persons wanting to give.

The gospel left a lonely hill and an empty tomb in Judea and reached all the way to Gaza.

Sitting here in a tire shop in Yakima, Washington, waiting for my tires to be changed, the signs of affluence all around me, I wonder about all of those wildly happy people who have no wealth and have much sickness. I see them dancing, praising, waving their meager notes [money] in the air, giving their offering. (This is called a hit-the-table offering, which can take up to two hours. People march to the front with their offering numerous times, dancing down the aisles and praising God. When they give their money, they slap or hit the table, thus the name.) What is it that enthuses them, that excites them, that causes them to give and give and give some more?

Counting offering on Sunday following flood

And then I think of Jesus, God's offering of love for a sadly broken and dying world. Jesus laid down His life and took upon himself the sin and suffering of the world. I'm beginning to understand a little bit better these wildly celebrating people. Jesus laid down His life voluntarily, and God raised Him. The gospel didn't stay hanging on the Cross, a tragic story of history. The borrowed tomb became the symbol of overwhelming joy. Resurrection!

The gospel left a lonely hill and an empty tomb in Judea and reached all the way to Gaza. The gospel has arrived. It's worth dancing for. It's worth giving for. It's resurrection. That's what makes people give and give and give and give some more. . . .

Reverie dissolves into reality as Doug and Elaine shoulder the load of ministering in present-day circumstances.

July 5, Xai Xai. . . . Elaine and I are back in Xai Xai, having returned here for repairs to the *JESUS* film projection equipment. Saturday we started out bright and early. In fact, as the sun flung its rays out over Gazaland, we were beginning our journey to Manjacaze. The back of the pickup was filled with *JESUS* film gear, two tents, food, clothing, everything to sustain a group of five to six persons for nine days in the bush. . . .

We arrived at Carateka around 1 P.M. A group of Christians had already gathered for this important event: the opening of a church that had been closed down by the forces of evil. Under the huge cashew trees, 45 Christians were singing and dancing and praising the Lord. "These doors were closed 24 years ago, but the gospel continued to spread out like these trees," they sang, raising their hands toward heaven.

Mary Cooper had planted this church some 40 years ago. I stood there watching the people, the sun's rays casting beams of light and cutting the shade of the cashew forest. In my mind's eye, I saw a young Mary walking this land, her life a gift for the Master. Churches, chapels, and persons witness to her faith, devotion, and commitment.

Lost in my thoughts, I was brought back to the present by a commotion. Someone was running toward us, coming out of the distant shadows. First, one young man and then another, yelling, calling out, "Who are you? Are you Nazarenes? Tell me, are you the Nazarenes?" A man named Roger fell on his knees, weeping.

"Why do you cry," I inquired.

"I was five when this place was closed, and it was announced that it would never open again, not for a thousand years. I prayed that Nazarenes would come back, and now my prayers have been answered."

The other young man arrived. "I thought this place might be closed forever." He looked to heaven and praised the One who "sent these Christians here."

We entered the building, singing praises, and heard four or five different sermons. This was followed by the installation of Martha Mabunda as pastor, following in the footsteps of Mary Cooper. When Elaine asked Martha about her life and dreams, she said, "My life is given over to Jesus. . . ."

6

Open Doors and Thank-Yous

How do missionaries and national leaders know which open doors to enter? How can one adequately say "thank-you" for the gospel? Perhaps we catch some insight into these hard-to-answer questions as we travel the African bush trails with Doug and Elaine via their personal computer.

September 12, remembered while on furlough. . . . Preaching outside the village of Chibuto in a reed-and-mud church building, I was impressed by the crowd that filled every square inch and flowed out under the large mango and canoe trees. Nearby the demon drums were pounding out a rhythm straight from the heart of hell. It was loud, almost over-whelming. Summoning our courage, we began to sing and expound on the death and resurrection of Jesus Christ and the power and cleansing from sin received through His precious blood. The demon drums became silent. It was eerie. Suddenly, a girl fell over, foaming at the mouth. Demons tore and convulsed her body. This young woman had been involved with witch doctors and Satan worship since she started attending a nearby boarding school. The elders took her outside and expelled the demons from her in Jesus' name. The gospel is proclaimed.

The miracle of Mozambique is simply the advance of the gospel through this unprecedented open door. An open door for the gospel. An open door that no man can shut! . . .

August 14, remembered from the vantage point of furlough. . . . "Turn here," the Mozambican said, indicating a large tree at the side of the dirt track we had been following for what seemed to be hours.

"Right here?" I asked incredulously, "but there is no road."

"Yes," he smiled, "we make our own road now."

We then followed an even more overgrown track, the bush and trees becoming thicker. I looked anxiously at my friend, concerned about the car and land mines. He just grinned. "Not to worry, missionary. We will arrive OK. Just fine."

In places the bush scraped both sides of the Toyota. Needles of acacia thorns clawed at the auto, trying to hinder us from reaching our destination. I shifted to four-wheel drive but felt there might be something wrong with a tire. Finding an open place in the dense brush, I stopped and checked the tires. A thorn had pierced the right front one. Fortunately, I had three spares in the back.

"Be careful, missionary," my companion warned.

The Perkinses' four-wheel-drive Toyota, an indispensable mission vehicle

"Here, there are very large snakes." I looked all around now, worried about serpents. Not seeing any, I proceeded to jack up the truck. My friend loosened the lug nuts while I watched for reptiles and other wild animals. We were on a mission to visit an old retired pastor. He lived in a forgotten corner of the bush a thousand miles from nowhere, and we knew he was sick with malaria.

As we pressed on, another flat. We had traveled 30 kilometers (18.5 miles) at the most. Watching for snakes, animals, and bandits, we changed this tire and resumed our journey. Now we were driving through the rugged bush with no track to follow. Anxiously, I looked over at my companion.

"The Lord will protect us," he said calmly.

Soon we saw it—smoke rising from the bush ahead. We pushed our way through the final thick clump of acacia trees and found ourselves in the middle of the homestead, a cleared out patch of sand 30 yards square. Chickens, pigs, goats, ducks, and dogs ran around—literally everywhere.

"The gospel, the gospel, the gospel, it has arrived."

The people were waiting for us. They had heard the truck coming for miles. As we broke through the wall of junglelike brush, the ebony-colored people in one voice broke into chorus.

"The gospel, the gospel, the gospel, it has arrived." It was almost a chant. They clapped, they danced, they broke out into smiles and laughter, and the women trilled their tongues. I looked around, and lying on a buffalo grass mat in the middle of the compound under a tree was a gray-haired man. He was shriveled with wrinkle lines marking every little place on his face. His eyes shone, though, and filled with tears.

"Oh, thank you, thank you," he kept saying. He took my hand and began to stroke it, like something new and precious. "I'm very sick but I prayed and the Lord sent you." His mouth was parched, and I called for some water to be brought from the pickup. I placed my hand under his head and lifted it partway and let cool water trickle down onto dried, cracked lips.

"Well, I heard you were ill and had no medicines, so I decided to come here," I told him.

"No, the Lord sent you," he insisted. *OK, the Lord sent me,* I thought. "Heh, heh," he chuckled, "the Lord sent you." It was the laugh of a man who joyfully knows that his Friend would never let him down. I gave this Christian gentleman some chloroquine tablets to fight the malaria that raged in his body.

"We must have a service," the old man insisted. People had begun to gather, sitting on grass mats under the canopy of huge cashew and mango trees. Children ran through the bush. Teenagers gathered. Young women nursed their infants, while men sat under the shade of the large trees. A snake scurried for its den.

The older women sang, then the younger women, then the men and boys. For two hours they sang. It was an impromptu service followed by an impromptu message. Fifty people came to seek forgiveness of sins. Four teens called on the name of the Lord for forgiveness. One, a demoniac, screamed out for mercy. In the name of Jesus, she was freed.

Four o'clock came, and we set our faces toward home. "Oh, thank you, thank you," the old man's words rang in our ears. "Thank you for the medicine. Thank you for coming to my home. Thank you for the gospel."

July 22, remembered on furlough. . . . After three hours of traveling at five miles per hour and negotiating endless miles of potholes, broken tar, and places where there was no road, Elaine and I finally arrived at the edge of the mighty, crocodile-infested Limpopo River. "Come," they had said, "please come and be with us. We've had no missionary here for over 30 years."

The pastor had promised that he would send a boat to ferry us across the river. A half mile across on the other side, we saw a boat starting over, a thin speck on the opposite bank. We watched for crocodiles. The small, precarious-looking boat arrived on our side. I watched in amazement as it was being poled by a 13-year-old boy. We stepped into the boat, more than a little anxious about the trip. Biceps bulging, the young teen pushed us ever deeper into the river flow. I looked back over my shoulder. The youth smiled. I noticed his teeth. He had them all, and they were very white.

"Are . . . are there any crocodiles in this river?" I ventured.

Our boatsman chuckled. "Many crocs. But, mahn, not to worry," he consoled me. "The last person to be eaten here was about two months ago when he fell out of this boat." Out of *this* boat? I looked back; he was still all smiles. "You know the pastor picked me because I'm the best one to bring you across. Don't worry, mahn!"

Arriving safely, Pastor Timothy greeted us. Tears moistened his eyes and cheeks as he embraced us. "Oh, thank you, thank you for coming." We walked toward the church (five miles away), a mud and thatch building. "We built it ourselves," Timothy said proudly.

The community was Guiza, meaning "place of

slaughter, place of the dead." "Here," the pastor pointed, "right here, the bodies were stacked 6 bodies high and 20 wide. There were so many, so many." He shook his head back and forth. "It took days for us to bury them all." His voice trembled, "They were our brothers."

The people sang, clapped, danced, and held their money high above their heads.

Then, somewhere up ahead, we heard it, faintly at first but stronger with each step forward. "There is power in the blood, power in the blood of Jesus." It rang out across the dull, dead land. A boy saw us and raced for the church in the distance, shouting as he ran.

When we arrived at the church, the people broke out into a tumult of choruses, dancing, and laughing. They called out, "There they are. They have come. Look at them." The people welcomed us. They touched our skin and felt Elaine's hair. "Oh, you are our brothers," they said, "and you have come."

A five-hour service followed with two hours for the hit-the-table offering alone. The people sang, clapped, danced, and held their money high above their heads. Special music, more singing, and then preaching. People sought forgiveness and repented. More singing. Another offering.

It was time to head for home as the sun, a red-orange disk, was beginning to sink in the western sky. Tall and short, thin and even thinner people stood in a long line, single file, and we walked past each one. They reached out their hands just to touch, to feel, to take in the texture of love.

One lady, the former town prostitute, the last in the line said, "They sent Jesus to us, and He arrived."

It was back to the boat and across the river to our Toyota and then four hours home.

You sent Jesus, and He arrived. You sent Life to the place of the dead. . . .

7

The Gospel Alive

*S*eedtime and harvest, the tears of intercessory prayer, the increase that only God can give— all are integral parts of the cycle of growing spiritual crops in Mozambique, both historically and presently. The gospel in this land is alive and well!

The Good News is spread through compassionate ministries, leadership training, extension education, evangelism, including the tool of the JESUS film. All these facets of the gospel appear to be woven seamlessly in the ministry robe of service that Doug and Elaine and the Mozambican leaders endeavor to wear and share.

Although they often encounter the fierce forces of evil, Doug's E-mail messages remind us that the battle is the Lord's. Moreover, "they that wait upon the LORD shall renew their strength" (Isaiah 40:31, KJV).

May 14, Xai Xai. . . . Elaine and I had a long trip up into Inhambane Province, filled with excitement and some disappointments, but the good far outweighed the bad. . . . One man even remembered you, Dad, from old Lourenço Marques days. He said, "When your father preached, he always gave us some vitamins. Now his son is here. Will he also give us some vitamins?" Well, I did my best. The gospel of the Lord Jesus is sweeping over the land.

I was touched in particular by the district superintendent, Pastor Mavilla. He left everything he had in Maputo—electric lights, car, house—to move to Vilankulos and lead the work there. He has no running water, no electricity, no car, and his house is just a simple two-room affair. He and his wife are up every morning at the crack of dawn, praying and asking God to supply their needs. They receive very little salary. This is what he said in his district superintendent's report: "Every day we trust the Lord for our daily bread, and every day our Lord supplies all of our needs." This from a man who receives virtually nothing. Their district grew over 100 percent this year alone. . . .

Nazarenes from the Inhambane Province

As we were driving home last evening, we came down through the baobab thickets. Some of those trees have been there for thousands of years. Off to the distant horizon, the sun, a red-orange ball, hung for a few minutes and then began to sink behind some dark, jagged clouds. And the Spirit seemed to be saying: "Go. Go to Vilankulos, Mabote, Mabelane, as far as the setting sun, preach the gospel." The gospel liberates and frees. . . .

June 3, Xai Xai. . . . Last night the demon drums beat all night. This has gone on for several nights in a row. It's all part of a ritual to appease ancestral spirits, which, in traditional thinking, can come back to haunt.

Yesterday I was up in Tavane, working on a water project. The community is using a well dug by the mission ages ago. They are using pipes laid by the mission, and now we are getting the entire community, which has burgeoned from 500 to over 2,500, to take responsibility for the maintenance and upkeep.

We are getting involved in a water buffalo project in the same area. Eventually, we will purchase water buffalo and breed them there. It is hoped that the people can then use the buffalo to pull plows and cultivate their lands. On the other hand, they will raise buffalo to provide cultivation animals for other pastors and communities. They will also use the milk to feed malnourished babies as well as make butter and cheese. . . .

June 6, Xai Xai. . . . Arising early, I left Elaine, although not really wanting to. Elaine had a bad back, and I was more than a little hesitant to leave her, although next to our home is a Church of the Nazarene with about 250 members. I was sure that they would look in on her.

I found the route to Chibuto, a tarred road and, therefore, no need of four-wheel drive. Arriving at 8:00 A.M., we ate breakfast, then prayed, and entered the church building. I began to marvel, as in 1996, the church was struggling with around 10 persons in attendance. Then they received a new pastor who is also the district superintendent. Today they had around 150 in Sunday School and close to 300 in church. After I preached in Portuguese with interpretation into Shangaan, more than 140 persons came forward at the invitation. Some were seeking to be sanctified; others were seeking salvation; still others wanted to recommit their lives to Jesus.

The pastor later advised all who still had things that belonged to Satan and witchcraft—such as cloths with magical properties, bracelets, and leg bands—to bring them to church and burn them. There could be no spiritual victory while the people kept things that belonged to Satan. We then baptized 11 persons and received them into the fellowship of believers. . . .

Arriving home, I worried at what I would find. But I shouldn't have. The church people had come over in a group and prayed for Elaine. "Raise our mother up, O Lord," they prayed, "so she can serve You with her husband. Stretch out Your hand as You did in Acts and heal her completely." And when I returned, their "mother" was up and was fixing some supper. The Lord had touched her. . . .

July 30, Xai Xai. . . . Today we begin preparation for the leadership conference to be held here at our home next week. We have to buy the food, check the airstrip, purchase wood to cook on, find accommodations, and prepare for a presentation on extension education. . . .

We are expecting Wes and Carolyn Taylor on Saturday. It will be so good to have them and a time to take some time off. Life can get pretty lonely and isolated here. Sometimes all we have to cling to is our God, His Word, a few photos, or Bach's "Minuet in G Minor" or "His Sheep May Safely Graze."

Extension center students taking a test

57

**It becomes sort of a duel of sounds—
a duel of the heart and the emotions.**

It's quite amusing to have the demon drums pounding through the night, frenzied, frantic rhythm flying through the palms and then to turn on Bach's "His Sheep May Safely Graze." It becomes sort of a duel of sounds—a duel of the heart and the emotions. In the places of sand, grinding poverty, sickness, and death, where nothing works properly and the modern world is a thousand miles away, His sheep may safely graze. In places where two-year-olds come and go like days of the calendar, death raising its grizzled head, His sheep may safely graze. In the places of loneliness, of silence, in the solitude of aloneness, His sheep may safely graze, led on by the Shepherd's gentle hand. A song for all time and the cadence changes, liltingly across the same rugged and torn landscape, crushing the mocking drums of death and demons, "Jesu, Joy of Man's Desiring." His sheep may safely graze. . . .

September 10, Xai Xai. . . . Our trips to Hokwe and Vilankulos went well, and we were able to accomplish quite a bit for the Kingdom. . . . In Vilankulos we showed the *JESUS* film for three nights in a row. The first night we had around 350 persons; the second evening, around 500-600; the third night, 1,000 or more. . . .

The first night, I saw a satellite make its way

across the heavens—a blue light winking on and off. The second night, I saw a shooting star that blazed across the heavens toward the north and fell toward the earth at about a 45-degree angle. Thursday night we had scorpions crawling around, two coming right toward Elaine and Dan Jones. On all the nights we had masses of persons coming forward to receive Christ and others to recommit their lives.

Elaine and I try to find something in the *JESUS* film every night that speaks to us. Last night it was Jesus' teaching that not one of Solomon's splendors could equal the splendor of one flower created by our Heavenly Father. It seemed to say to us that we can trust our Father's perfect will for our loved ones in Casa Robles, for those leaving for distant lands, and for our children in college.

Thursday evening, two men stood and played musical instruments. One played the guitar; the other, the clarinet. The word of inspiration went out from our Father and put music into these two Africans. The man on the clarinet was absolutely sensational. They played and sang about God's care and love for us. We sat enthralled as music poured forth under the starry firmament—"God Will Take Care of You"—a message from the Father's heart. . . .

September 19, Xai Xai. . . . Our Lord's Day began with our travel out to Chinunguine, a distance of 12 kilometers (7.5 miles). Arriving at 10:00 A.M., we began a two-hour church service. . . . I preached a simple message on having faith in Jesus. Many children and 28 adults came forward to pray. Many women wept for a long time as they prayed out to God. Their lives are so difficult. The years are unrelenting as is their work. They age quickly. Afterward, they were so happy that they danced for about half an hour, singing one song of praise to the Lord about 50 or 60 times.

After lunch of chicken and rice, Elaine and I hurried home and got the *JESUS* film equipment and rushed back at 4:00 to the same church. As the sun began to slowly set behind the distant western hills, the church people began to sing. People began to show up—250 soon became 450 and then swelled to over 600. The film began. Suddenly, a group of raucous youth arrived. The pastor told us that a gang of young people were sent to disrupt the film. We prayed through the whole film. The film equipment worked perfectly. Even though the thugs were noisy, the film's volume pretty much drowned out their din.

As soon as the invitation was made to receive Christ, many of the youth ran off into the night. Chinunguine is known to be a difficult place, one of thugs and demonism. Some made a commitment to Christ, but the response was not like we have had in other places with hundreds or even thousands coming forward. Our plans are to return to this area and evangelize again, so that all of the strongholds of Satan might come down. . . .

October 3, Xai Xai. . . . Had a wonderful extension meeting last night. We showed the *JESUS* film, and a spirit of prayer came over the 21 persons present. It was unlike anything I've encountered yet. As it was very quiet in the room after the showing, I called the students to prayer. We all knelt and everyone started to pray. We prayed in a hushed, subdued tone for 10 minutes, and then the pastor of the local church prayed. He started off quietly, but got louder and louder, crying out to God for himself, the students, and his people. It was an awesome experience. . . .

When the church service started today, the building was packed, perhaps 550 to 600 persons crammed into the building. Persons were standing on the outside under the shade of trees. . . . The king of Xai Xai, the actual monarch of Xai Xai, came by to see the pastor of the church and waited out under the trees. The offering was huge—R600 (U.S.$100). People praised the Lord. . . .

When the appeal was given, 300 persons gathered around the altar. One woman cried out to the Lord to sanctify her. Another woman asked the Lord for courage to follow him in every situation. . . . One gentleman placed everything on the altar—his money, his employment, and finally himself.

Major discovery—ants! Everywhere we looked, millions, if not billions, of tiny, red ants.

It all began last night in the extension class when we showed the *JESUS* film to the students. There was such a spirit of brokenness among them. Many of them have volunteered to be a part of the *JESUS* film team and to go out and evangelize. . . .

October 24, Xai Xai. . . . Elaine and I just returned from a *JESUS* film campaign in the district of Chaimite. . . . For some reason, they have latched on-to Elaine and me and treat us as if we were their children. When we arrived in Chaimite, we greeted the people in the typical formal Shangaan way. Then we excused ourselves and looked for a place to erect our sleeping tent.

Major discovery—*ants!* Everywhere we looked, millions, if not billions, of tiny, red ants. We finally found a fairly level place, just five yards from the cattle corral, and set up the tent. We tried to find a place where the water would drain quickly in case of rain.

Ants. We were never without them. Ants in our pockets. Ants in our shoes. Ants in our ears. Ants everywhere, and nothing killed these ants. You kill a million with poison, and another million immediately take their place. That is understatement, not an exaggeration.

The tent up, we immediately began setting up the *JESUS* film equipment. People began coming. The sun went down. Here and there you would see groups of 2 or 3 or 7 come, melting in from the night. The crowd swelled to 800, maybe more.

Oohs and aahs undulated through the crowd as they reacted with joy when they saw Baby Jesus in mother Mary's arms. They called out the disciples' names as Jesus named them. But as Jesus called out the name Judas Iscariot, the people clicked their tongues to demonstrate their sheer disgust at the traitor in the midst of the disciples.

The Crucifixion. The silence was deafening. A

crowd of 800 and not a sound was uttered. Not a child stirred. A lone woman began to weep. It's the death wail—a lonely, sad funeral dirge in the black Chaimite night, a dirge played out in real time and real life every day in this area. Death stalks this barren plain.

The district superintendent shut off the *JESUS* film projector and started his appeal. Recapitulating the message of the film, he extended the offer of free salvation to all who would receive God's offer of forgiveness. A huge crowd pressed forward. The minister's voice blasted through the night over the public-address system. But the prayers of the throng, persons calling on the name of Jesus, almost drowned him out.

At the close of the prayer, the district superintendent explained the whole gospel again. He then invited those who wanted to be followers of Jesus to come forward and give their names and addresses. Around 80 did so. They are the basis of our follow-up.

We started the film where it was stopped. Jesus is placed in the tomb. A murmur of joy rippled through the crowd as He is raised from the dead and presents himself to the disciples.

When the film was over, the crowd melted away into the night. Supper was at 10:30, and an hour later Elaine and I were in our tent. No ants except from our clothes. We tried to shake and dust them off. . . .

The next evening we set up the film equipment again—a repeat of the night before. Three persons with demons came forward. The demons threw them to the ground. The Christians gathered around. After much prayer and calling on the name of Jesus, two of the women were liberated. One woman, the wife of the Zionist leader in the area, was not freed, and we continue to pray for her.

The hand of the Lord was manifest in Chaimite . . . hearts were open to the gospel. We praise the name of Jesus. . . .

8

Then the Floods Came

*T*he E-mails from Xai Xai for the first several months of the new millennium were dominated with firsthand reports of the worst flood in Mozambique in 50 years and its aftermath. The story that unfolded was more than tragedy, though; it included the gift of God's great grace and the helping hands of nations, relief agencies, and persons around the globe who reached out and touched Mozambicans in distress.

February 13, Xai Xai. . . . Elaine and I had a wonderful Lord's day right here where we live. We attended the church next door, and as is the custom they asked the missionary to preach. With around 550 in attendance, I was searching in my heart for something to preach about. It was a daunting task.

The Limpopo River is threatening to fill Xai Xai with water, the road to Maputo has been blocked, groceries are running out quickly, everyone has lost all of their harvest for the next six months, starvation is looming. Malaria and other ravaging diseases are spreading like wildfire. What to preach on this fine Sunday morning—this resurrection day?

Flood water slowly creeping into Xai Xai

People waiting to cross the flooded Limpopo River

The Holy Spirit led me to Luke 4:13-28 where Jesus was severely tempted in the desert by the devil, but the Holy Spirit helped Him to overcome. I then retold the story about Elijah and the widow whose meal and oil never ran out. . . .

Before I could finish my message, a girl came to the altar, then another, and soon the whole altar was lined. People called on the name of Jesus, just wanting to know that in their time of desperation, desolation, devastation, in their time of staggering want, their precious Savior would be with them.

Keep us in your prayers. We will stay here as long as possible and have absolutely no plans to evacuate. Our prayers are not necessarily to be delivered from suffering, but for our God to sustain us in all situations. Jesus increase our faith!

By this time, we had picked up South Africa news reports on the Internet, giving the death toll at 48 in Mozambique after two weeks of torrential rains. International agencies and the United Nations were beginning to mobilize and provide emergency supplies and food for flood victims numbering in the hundreds of thousands. Others were trying to assess health needs. Individual countries, such as the United States, Portugal, and other European states, pledged money. South Africa was deploying helicopters to fly on relief missions. Nazarene news sources began to carry specific prayer requests for missionaries and Mozambican Nazarenes affected by the floodwaters.

February 18, Xai Xai. . . . Reprieve. The floodwater as of this morning has not breached the Xai Xai floodwall. The rural areas are totally devastated. People are up in trees and on the roofs of their huts. The water has swept many of them away.

The rising waters are also bringing out the snakes. . . . One mamba snake entered a hut and killed everyone inside—eight in all! . . .

February 20, Xai Xai. . . . Today we had a four-hour service with around 500 persons present. There was a sense of the presence of the Lord. One man who had been stranded by the rising water brought the roof down with his rendition of "He Giveth More Grace." Every song, every testimony, every prayer all pointed to the indomitable spirit of the people and their unshakable faith in Jesus Christ. . . .

February 22, Xai Xai. . . . We have a large group of refugees with us, and I took them downtown to buy food. Interestingly enough, a truck had just arrived with a load of rice, its precious cargo shipped from California. It was the last truck to come through before the road to Beira was cut by Cyclone Eline. People are in desperate and dire straits. Out in the floodwaters, persons are stranded in trees and on their rooftops. Dead cattle and carcasses are floating in the floodwaters. Fishermen have been out rescuing persons. One man brought in 39 persons and went back out for more. . . .

By February 23, Nazarene Compassionate Ministries sent out a bulletin on the Mozambique flood, requesting prayer and support. The Africa *regional office released $27,000 to begin the relief process. Nazarenes—individuals and churches—around the world began to respond with prayer and cash. And the flooding continued.*

February 24, Xai Xai. . . . We are receiving a resupply from the mission tomorrow. They are bringing in food and fuel on a helicopter. Be in prayer. The helicopter should land about a mile from our house. When a helicopter came in two days ago across the river, a huge mob gathered and literally stole and ripped every bag of rice apart. These are desperate times. Keep your news coming through, as we need a sense of normalcy! It must be normal somewhere in the world. God is our Rock! . . .

February 25, Xai Xai. . . . Last October Elaine and I spent five days roughing it in the bush at Changenine. We left with heavy hearts because there was so little response to the gospel. Today we received a shocking message. All of central and much of southern Mozambique is underwater. What about Changenine? Gone. Wiped out by the floods. Not a dry place anywhere. Totally underwater, several meters deep. Many persons drowned. And we never knew it!

"I have lost everything," she said, "but I haven't lost my Jesus, and He hasn't lost me."

That was the last chance we had to share the gospel with many of the people there. I was hoping for one more opportunity. . . . Every day 15 to 20 hungry refugees come to our home expecting to be fed; 17 of them are sleeping here every night. The football stadium in Xai Xai is packed with refugees, as are the schools.

One elderly woman, her face weather-beaten, etched with lines of worry, held my hand. Tears flowed from her eyes. "I have lost everything," she said, "but I haven't lost my Jesus, and He hasn't lost me." Water stretches to the horizon. We are almost an island on a large sea. . . .

By the end of February, Xai Xai was completely underwater. No one had electricity, water, or fuel in the area. Doug and Elaine elected to stay to help with the refugees and to assist Daniel Jones, the Nazarene Mission Aviation director for Africa, and Anton Hol, another Nazarene pilot, in their efforts to get supplies delivered from Nazarene Compassionate Ministries (NCM). News reports indicated that the South African Air Force had rescued 8,000 people after the latest wave of floods, but another 100,000 were stranded. Photos of the flood became a part of newscasts and newspapers around the world. The aid response became global.

March 1, Xai Xai. . . . The generator you purchased for us some years ago is the only thing that enables us to send and receive E-mail. Thank you for that. . . .

Helimission, a nondenominational group,
helping to deliver supplies from NCM.

Flooded stores in downtown Xai Xai

Elaine and I actually had a "good" day and are praising the Lord for His mercies. Several helicopter flights brought 2,000 pounds of food. The food supplies were purchased with funding from NCM and go toward feeding the refugees and homeless persons.

Suspension bridge over Limpopo River near Xai Xai

The floodwaters are continuing to rise. In fact they are threatening to engulf the rest of Xai Xai, reaching up the hill to where we live. We're keeping watch on the waters every night. They still have 60 feet to climb. Many of our neighbors and church people will go under the flood this evening. We are sur-

rounded by water and have only two escape routes—
one to the beach and the other to the north.

The days that lie ahead will be very difficult as
we find out who is missing. We have just gone
through the grieving process following the civil war,
and now will come the grieving after the flood of
the millennium. We find ourselves grieving in so
many ways. . . .

*Then unexpectedly a welcomed E-mail note came
from pilot Daniel Jones:*

March 2, Swaziland. . . . Just wanted to let you
know that I saw Doug and Elaine yesterday. They
are in good spirits and hanging in there. We flew in
one ton of rice, maize, beans, sugar, salt, milk pow-
der, diesel, petrol, cooking gas, canned goods, medicines, and even some Oreos and popcorn. We had to
shuttle the food by helicopter from the closest
airstrip. They have access to a cell phone, and we're
going to try to get them a satellite phone by the
weekend. I'll be going back to Maputo tomorrow to
help fly more relief aid to various towns. The relief
effort is growing by the day, with many large cargo
aircraft landing and off-loading huge amounts of
food. . . .

*By March 3, the E-mails detailed more of the suf-
fering. The district superintendent from Chibuto
had called to say they were totally out of food
without any means to buy some. One of the pastors had been without food for quite awhile and*

his wife and children were desperately sick. Elaine called Dan Jones and arranged for food and cash to be delivered, all courtesy of NCM. Doug and Elaine were surviving on one meal a day by that time.

The March 3 issue of Nazarene News Summary *carried a story "A Tidal Wave of Misery in Mozambique":*

March 3, *Nazarene News.* . . . A massive wall of water about six feet high came roaring down the Limpopo River early Monday morning and slammed into an area of Mozambique already devastated with two weeks of storms. . . . Xai Xai, a city of 70,000 people, is completely submerged, and dozens of other towns and villages are totally underwater. . . . There are over 50,000 Nazarenes in Mozambique, many of whose safety is not known at this time. . . . "This is a monumental tragedy, a tragedy of epic proportions," said Nazarene missionary Doug Perkins. . . . "There are hundreds of thousands of people, many of them Nazarenes, who are left destitute in the wake of this disaster. . . ."

The following day, Doug and Elaine were well into the aid distribution phase of the disaster. Meeting Nazarene planes in Chibuto, organizing trucks for hauling supplies and food, securing nurses and technicians and training them to administer the medical packs, lining up church people of various denominations to channel aid to the most needy, getting volunteers to meet and care for refugees as they staggered off the rescue helicopters, all this—and more—became part of Doug and Elaine's exhausting "routine."

Refugee camp in Chibuto with a population of 85,000 at its peak

Bob Prescott, director of NCM, personally visited Mozambique in March. Joerg Eich from Germany went for six weeks to supervise the NCM flood relief efforts. He was later relieved by Heinz Schubert, a retired South African lay volunteer. Another $50,000 was released from Compassionate Ministries funds for flood relief and Nazarenes around the globe began to mobilize in earnest to help their brothers and sisters in need.

E-mails for those beginning days of March were filled with spectacular miracles and answers to

Heinz Schubert, director of relief operations

prayer—of finding Nazarene leaders safe, of airlifting newborns and relatives, of almost instant responses to prayer for ways and means to get food to stranded people. For example, one morning a French helicopter pilot came up to Doug and asked in English if there was a village in particular that needed food. Doug told him, "Chaimite." Doug wrote:

March 6, Xai Xai. . . . Just this morning Elaine and I had a good cry. We asked the Lord to help us get food to our brothers in Chaimite. They had been without food for days. Many of our pastors there are young and recently ordained to the ministry. One was married just two months ago. The Lord answered our prayer at exactly 8:00 this morning. Thanks to the French Air Force and the strong arm of the Lord. . . .

Some of 2,000 refugees waiting for medical attention

In the midst of the chaotic days and nights of helping aid refugees, Doug and Elaine both became seriously ill—Elaine with a virus and Doug with double pneumonia. The German doctors who had arrived in the area were immediately available to diagnose and administer adequate medication, however. And God provided rest and healing even on the front lines of the battle.

Bob Prescott's assessment of the Mozambique crisis came in a March 14 press release:

March 14, *Nazarene News.* . . . The crisis is awful and awesome—74 temporary camps with over 300,000 people waiting to return home. . . . Many are sitting or standing in the rain, hoping for delivery of food by relief helicopters. The best crops in years are gone underwater.

Compassion wins! When people see God's love manifested through the caring assistance of His Church . . . they will be attracted to the gospel.

Nazarene losses are still unassessed. . . . All district superintendents have now been accounted for, but there is no report on pastors and Nazarene members and their families. At least 36 churches on 7 districts are affected, but there is no report on their condition. . . . But, the good news is . . . God has a plan for building His church in Mozambique! I firmly believe that. I liken His plan to a picture puzzle with many pieces. Our job is to help locate the pieces and fit them together with the guidance of the Holy Spirit. . . .

The Church of the Nazarene in Mozambique has been growing rapidly over the past several years, now totaling 31 districts and 50,000 members. Some fear that this physical, financial, and personal disaster for so many will curtail continued growth. I believe otherwise. Compassion wins! When people see God's love manifested through the caring assistance of His Church and its members, I believe they will be attracted to the gospel. . . .

> *That is exactly what began to happen. Doug and Elaine's E-mail began to reflect the revival that was coming to Mozambique. In spite of or because of the floodwaters, God was sending showers of blessing to His people and church along the Limpopo River.*

March 15, Xai Xai. . . . A family thought to be lost in the flood showed up on Sunday at the Xai Xai City church. The church, 750 strong, had a spontaneous praise service. One man stood to his feet and confessed that he was not living the way that he should be. He had demon rags in his home. He had been up to the home of the great witch doctor of the area and had knelt before him, selling his soul to Satan. Sunday he knelt before Christ and confessed all, and a spirit of revival broke out.

In spite of the many hardships, loss, and grief, we have heard that in other churches the same spirit is evident. Spontaneous offerings—hit-the-table offerings—have broken out.

One pastor stood to his feet and proclaimed that these floods were sent by Satan to stop the work of the Lord from progressing. He declared, "Though Mozambicans are suffering tremendously, we will never turn our backs on our faith and on our

Christ." He called for an immediate hit-the-table offering, and the people gave a year's wage. . . .

March 24, Xai Xai. . . . A sad note. A lady came to
church for the first time on Sunday. Monday she
drowned on her way into Xai Xai in a little boat.
Her funeral was today. Judgment has fallen on many
persons. There is a terrible fear upon the church at
the moment, something akin to the awe of God's divine presence and an awareness of His judgment and
intolerance of sin. People are taking stock of their
lives. They are realizing that you can't live a double
life. Soon you come under the judgment of God. . . .

*Even as the unseasonable rains continued and
Doug and Elaine were cut off from the outside
world except for air transportation and E-mail,
their ministry continued to function in the refugee
camps and through the JESUS film. Nearby, crocodiles, hippos, snakes—disturbed by the floodwaters—made themselves more visible than usual.*

*In the meantime, NCM personnel were busily
sending aid to refugees. World Mission Division
Director Louie Bustle stated, "This is the largest relief effort in the history of Nazarene Compassionate Ministries."*

*The late May and early June reports from
Kansas City and Johannesburg on the Mozambique flood indicated NCM was moving beyond
the crisis phase of recovery into restoration and de-
velopment. By this time over $950,000 had been
donated, including more than $100,000 from Ger-*

*many. Prayer was requested for the district and lo-
cal church leaders who would begin to assume the
major responsibility for the continuing relief efforts.*

*By mid-June, it became apparent that the im-
mediate response by the Church of the Nazarene
had made a lasting impression in southern
Mozambique. From government officials to farmers
to refugees, Mozambicans recognized the symbol of
the church, according to Joanie Doerr of Nazarene
Communications News Africa:*

June 25, *Out of Africa* news. . . . During the devas-
tating floods in Mozambique, the gospel was
preached from unusual and precarious pulpits. Missionary Doug Perkins visited the Chokwe area this
month, where the district headquarters is situated.
Located on the flood plain of the Limpopo River,
Chokwe is the town that was struck by a raging wall
of water at 2:00 A.M. on February 28. Rev. Daniel
Munguambe, district superintendent of the Limpopo
District, told Perkins that he held tightly to his Bible
as he and his family scrambled to climb a tree.
Perkins said: "Having his Bible with him, Munguambe began to preach. He called on the people to repent of their sin and to trust in Jesus to forgive them
and to deliver them." Munguambe now has a reputa-
tion in Chokwe as "the pastor who called from the
treetops for the people to repent!" Recently, he had
one of the converts from a nearby tree thank him for
bringing her the gospel.

Perkins reported visiting the Chokwe Church of
the Nazarene on June 18. According to Perkins, the

church was crowded to capacity with people standing on the outside looking in. At the close of the service, a woman who had been bound by demons for 25 years was delivered by the power of Jesus' name. Commenting on this vibrant, growing church, Perkins said, "There was an exciting spirit of hope and trust in the Lord."

About this time, a 20-foot overseas shipping container filled with FAM-PAKS and MedCare Paks left Miami for Maputo. The huge project involved the entire Southeast U.S.A. Region where local, district, and general levels of the NWMS (now NMI) mobilized and coordinated their efforts in a very short time frame. The distance between the helpless and the helpers became shorter. The God of all comfort was at work.

The Chibuto Central Church ran 400 before flooding; now it is running over 800.

July 10, Xai Xai. . . . People have wondered what life is like postflood. The roads, bridges, and infrastructures were smashed to pieces. The rain persists, and so we have to constantly be aware of whether the roads are open or closed. Cholera is reported to be breaking out in isolated and distant communities. Prices of food and building materials are high.

We've had the privilege of attending three district assemblies in the past two weeks. Growth on the districts most affected by the floodwaters has been phenomenal. The Chibuto Central Church ran 400 before flooding; now it is running over 800. The 25th of June Church had 50 before the flood and is now over 350. A sense of revival has swept our churches here in Gaza.

Thank you for the thousands of dollars given to Nazarene Compassionate Ministries. Hundreds of families have been helped, homes rebuilt, and churches repaired. Many are participating in the Work for Food program. Thank you! . . .

And, in Out of Africa, *Joanie Doerr reported:*

August 13, Johannesburg. . . . The *JESUS* film team from Xai Xai, Mozambique, recently visited a brand new village known as "Village 2000." This village is located just outside of Xai Xai. Most of the people in the village are flood victims, who lost their homes, possessions, and gardens. The *JESUS* film is being used to plant a new church among these people. Missionary Doug Perkins reports: "This new church is a daughter church of the Inhamissa Church of the Nazarene in Xai Xai. The Inhamissa Church has commissioned their assistant pastor to be the pastor of the new Village 2000 church."

The Mozambique Area One district assemblies have been completed. According to missionary Doug Perkins, all the districts showed growth in the double digits of percentage. Perkins stated: "There has been a great spirit of thanksgiving and praise in spite of the flooding. At the Chokwe assembly, a young pastor's wife stood and gave this testimony: 'I thank God for the floods. Through them God has brought even more persons to himself.' This testimony of grace is from a lady who lost her home and all of her possessions."

> *Mozambique Moments were full of God's love and grace. Although some of those moments were clouded by floodwaters, God's rainbow of promise held true!*
>
> *The computer is turned off; the Internet connection is lost. But the cycle of ministry in Mozambique continues . . . the showing of the JESUS film in the bush . . . the medical teams working in Tavane . . . the leadership conferences held in Xai Xai . . . the extension classes taught in makeshift classrooms across the districts . . . the Lord's Day services held in Alabaster churches or under the spreading trees.*
>
> *And the Lord of the Harvest calls to us again —in all parts of the world—to pray, to go, to give —until He comes again.*

Epilogue
The Vision Transmitted

The generations of Nazarenes—both missionary and African—continue to share the gospel vision in Mozambique.

Yesterday, Floyd Perkins answered God's call, arriving in Mozambique in 1952 to open the work among the Portuguese. Later, his young Shangaan secretary was Jonas Mulate, whose father, Lot Mulate, was one of the early African district superintendents.

Elaine and Doug Perkins with their daughter Elise and husband, David Mosher. Doug is holding granddaughter, Esther Renee Kanya, born in February 2001.

Today, Jonas is an African regional missionary from Mozambique to Angola. And his long-time contemporary, Doug Perkins, son of Floyd, is a missionary in Xai Xai, Mozambique, assigned there in 1994.

Tomorrow? Elise Perkins, one of Doug's daughters, is married to David Mosher, another MK (missionary kid) from Mozambique. Both Elise and David feel called by God and are preparing for missionary service.

And what of other youth, other children and teens, other young adults all around the world who are hearing the call to serve?

Each generation builds on the vision of the generation past. Through the Mozambican mosaic screen, the Great Commission is filtered, obeyed again, and transmitted with the same sense of urgency. The vision spills over the borders of Mozambique and is sometimes beamed electronically. But by whatever means it reaches us, the divine impulse to pray and give and go finds us all around the globe. And we respond!

Pronunciation Guide

Alta Shangaan	AHL-tuh shahng-GAHN
bava	BAH-vah
Beira	BEH-ruh
Carateka	kar-uh-TEH-kuh
Chaimite	shie-MEE-tee
Changenine	shahng-gah-NEE-nee
Chibuto	shee-BOO-toh
Chidingele	shee-deeng-GAY-leh
Chinunguine	shee-noon-GWEE-nee
Chokwe	SHOHK-way
Gaza	GAH-zuh
Guiza	gee-ZHAH
Hokwe	HOHK-way
Inhambane	een-yahm-BAH-nee
Inhamissa	een-yahm-MEE-sah
inkosikasi	in-KOH-see-KAH-see
Limpopo	lihm-POH-poh
Lourenço Marques	loh-REHN-zoh MAHRKS
Mabelane	mah-bay-LAH-nee
Mabote	mah-BOH-tee
Mabunda	mah-BOON-dah
mafureira	mah-foo-REH-rah
Manjacaze	mahn-jah-CAH-zee
Manzini	mahn-ZEE-nee
Maputo	mah-POO-too
Mavengane	mah-vay-NGAH-nee
Mavilla	mah-VEE-lah
mufundisi	mm-foon-DEE-see
Mulate	moo-LAH-tee
Munguambe	moong-GWAHM-beh
Shangaan	shahng-GAHN
Tavane	tah-VAH-nee
Vilankulos	vee-lahng-KOO-loosh
Xai Xai	SHIE SHIE
Zavala	zah-VAH-lah